DISCOVERY ATLAS

Written by Anita Ganeri
Illustrated by Sara Lynn Cramb

Quarto is the authority on a wide range of topics.

Quarto educates, entertains and enriches the lives of our readers—enthusiasts and lovers of hands-on living.

www.quartoknows.com

A catalogue record for this book is available from the British Library.

Author: Anita Ganeri
Illustration and Design: Sara Lynn Cramb
Consultant: Martin Darlison
Project Editor: Nancy Dickmann
Editorial Director: Laura Knowles
Art Director: Susi Martin
Publisher: Maxime Boucknooghe

ISBN: 978-1-78493-780-5

Printed and bound in China

10 9 8 7 6 5 4 3 2 1   16 17 18 19 20

Acknowledgements

The publisher thanks the following agencies for their kind permission to use their images.
Key: bg = background, t = top, b = bottom, l = left.
r = right, c = centre.

Alamy: 15tr Kumar Sriskandan, 27t Avalon/Photoshot License, 39tl BasilT, 47t Janzig/CentralAsia; Getty: 59t Whitworth Images, 61b Doug Allan; Shutterstock: 8t Chris Geszvain, 8m Ammit Jack, 9b hessianmercenary, 9t Aivolie, 10l Brent Hofacker, 10r Mike Zakharov, 11t bikeriderlondon, 11r Fotokvadrat, 11b Tania Thomson, 12t momente, 12b logoboom, 13t UbjsP, 13m critterbiz, 13b Orhan Cam, 14t Anna Omelchenko, 14b AGCuesta, 15l Richard Goldberg, 15mr Oliver Hoffmann, 15b Matt Ragen, 16tl Alice Nerr, 16b KKulikov, 17t Fotos593, 17m kavram, 17b snowway, 18 Fotos593, 19tl Pablo Rogat, 19tm Marco Alhelm, 19r Elzbieta Sekowska, 19b saiko3p, 20tl Alf Ribeiro, 20b Roman Stetsyk, 21l sunsinger, 21tr Filipe Frazao, 22t Nebojsa Markovic, 22b theskaman306, 23l GUDKOV ANDREY, 23m GUDKOV ANDREY, 23r Volodymyr Burdiak, 24 stormarn, 25b Pascal RATEAU, 25t WitR, 25ml Pichugin Dmitry, 25mr Daniel Fleck, 26t Anton_Ivanov, 26l Yakov Oskanov, 26r Fer Gregory, 27t Aleksandar Todorovic, 27b Chantal de Bruijne, 28t StanislavBeloglazov, 28ml Bjoern Wylezich, 28mr giannimarchetti, 28b DK samco, 29t BarryTuck, 29r David Thyberg, 30t Valentina Photo, 30m ZinaidaSopina, 30b Wead, 31t Erik Mandre, 31b Patryk Kosmider, 32t muratart, 32b Kiko Jimenez, 33tl Lukas Gojda, 33tr Mariia Golovianko, 33b Rich Lynch, 34tl WDG Photo, 34tr Katja El Sol, 34m Jeannette Meier Kamer, 34bl Brendan Howard, 35tr Alexander Raths, 35b Naumenko Aleksandr, 36t V. Belov, 36r Norbert1986, 36l Alan Smillie, 37t Samot, 37bl Mariia Masich, 37br jasrim, 38l Karl Allgaeuer, 38r Aleksandar Todorovic, 39m nikolay100, 39br Dziurek, 40t Mikael Hjerpe, 40m MarinaDa, 40bl Palette7, 40br Sergey Petrov, 41 ALEKSANDR RIUTIN, 42t Bon Appetit, 42b Galyna Andrushko, 43t Mikhail Markovskiy, 43m Stationidea, 43b Hung Chung Chih, 44t WichitS, 44mr irisphoto1, 44ml ZouZou, 44b Seleznev Oleg, 45 Vladimir Melnik, 46t Natalia Davidovich, 46ml FotograFFF, 46mr AS Food studio, 46b Rudra Narayan Mitra, 47b Marina Khlybova, 48t Christian Bertrand, 48rm Perfect Lazybones, 48l Bavorndej, 48br David Evison, 49t India Picture, 49b Dmitry Strizhakov, 50t SIHASAKPRACHUM, 50b QiuJu Song, 51r J. Henning Buchholz, 51l Anton_Ivanov, 51b ChameleonsEye, 52t Joney, 52b Songsak Pandet, 53tr Tom Roche, 53l Rat007, 53b snowhite, 54tr Brian Kinney, 54tl FiledIMAGE, 54b worldswildlifewonders, 55t wong yu liang, 55b Pichugin Dmitry, 56t mark Higgins, 56b Nicotombo, 57t Neale Cousland, 57m Pumpchn, 57b ChameleonsEye, 58t Amy Nichole Harris, 58b Martin Valigursky, 59bl ChameleonsEye, 59br Jirsak, 60t Sergey Krasnoshchokov, 60m Female Traveller, 60b Christopher Wood, 61t I. Noyan Yilmaz, 61m TravelMediaProductions; Wikimedia Commons: 20m Cmacauley/ Wikimedia Commons.

CONTENTS

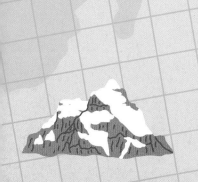
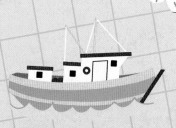

OUR WORLD

Do you enjoy an adventure? Are you ready to go exploring? You are about to go on a journey right around our world. In this book, you will visit some of the most fascinating places on Planet Earth, and meet the amazing people and wildlife that live there.

Land covers about a third of Planet Earth. Water and ice cover the rest. The land is split into seven main chunks. They are called the continents.

As you explore the book, look out for fast facts about each region.

Equator

The Equator is an imaginary line around the middle of the world. Everything below the line is in the south and everything above is in the north.

NORTH AMERICA

SOUTH AMERICA

FAST FACTS

Biggest continent: Asia
Coldest continent: Antarctica
Continent with most countries: Africa
Continent with most people: Asia

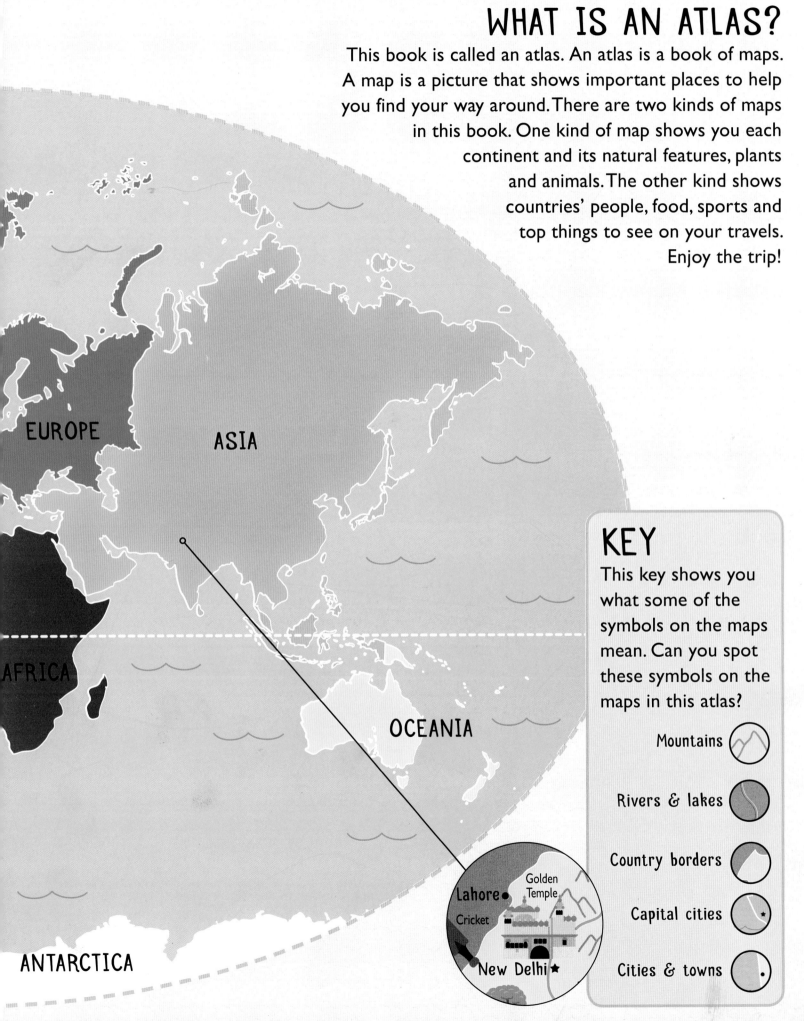

WHAT IS AN ATLAS?

This book is called an atlas. An atlas is a book of maps. A map is a picture that shows important places to help you find your way around. There are two kinds of maps in this book. One kind of map shows you each continent and its natural features, plants and animals. The other kind shows countries' people, food, sports and top things to see on your travels. Enjoy the trip!

EUROPE

ASIA

AFRICA

OCEANIA

ANTARCTICA

KEY

This key shows you what some of the symbols on the maps mean. Can you spot these symbols on the maps in this atlas?

Mountains

Rivers & lakes

Country borders

Capital cities

Cities & towns

Lahore
Golden Temple
Cricket
New Delhi ★

WHAT'S A BIOME?

Different places around the world have different sorts of weather. Places can be mostly hot or cold, wet or dry, or a mixture of all of these. These differences affect the kinds of plants and animals that can live there. A biome (say *bye*-ome) is a mixture of the weather, plants and animals found in a place. The different colours on the continent maps in this book show the different biomes.

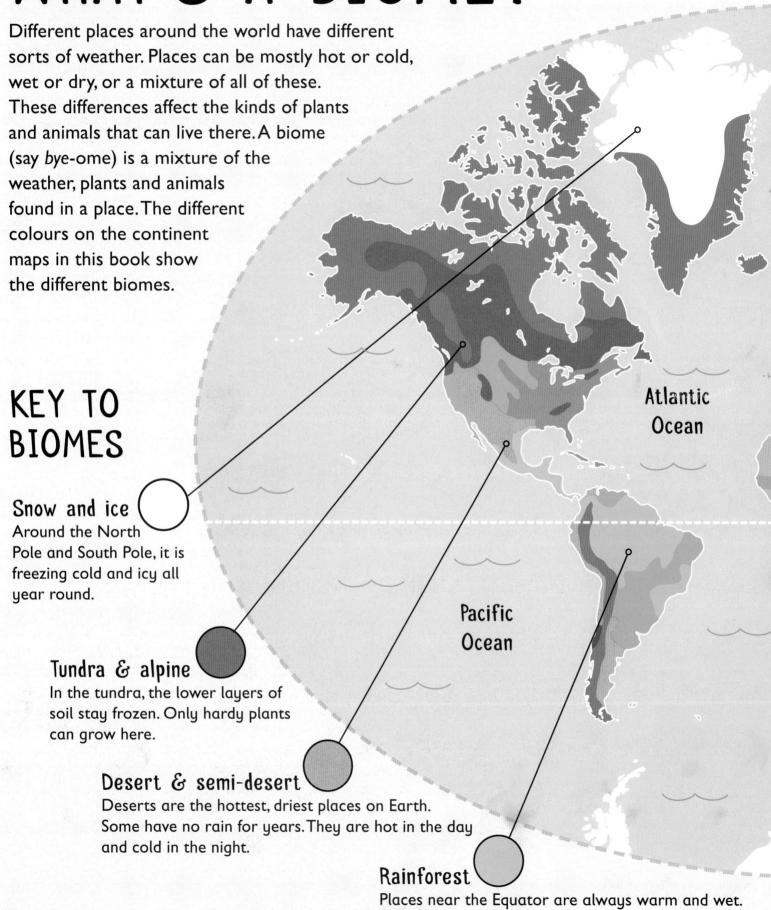

KEY TO BIOMES

Snow and ice
Around the North Pole and South Pole, it is freezing cold and icy all year round.

Tundra & alpine
In the tundra, the lower layers of soil stay frozen. Only hardy plants can grow here.

Desert & semi-desert
Deserts are the hottest, driest places on Earth. Some have no rain for years. They are hot in the day and cold in the night.

Rainforest
Places near the Equator are always warm and wet. Thick rainforests grow here.

Atlantic Ocean

Pacific Ocean

SALTY WATER

Salty sea water covers more than two thirds of the Earth. It fills the five oceans. The salt in the water comes from rocks on land. Rivers and the rain wash it into the sea.

Arctic Ocean

On your journey through the atlas, look out for icons that highlight each country's food, sport, culture, landmarks and more.

Equator

Indian Ocean

Southern Ocean

Conifer forest
Huge conifer forests stretch across the far north where winters are long and cold.

Deciduous forest
Deciduous forests are made of trees that lose their leaves in winter.

Grassland & savannah
Grasslands are huge, dry plains, covered in tall grasses, low trees and shrubs.

Shrubland
These are rocky areas with small shrubs. The summers are hot and dry, and the winters are rainy.

NORTH AMERICA

North America is a huge continent with 53 countries. The biggest is Canada. The smallest is St Kitts and Nevis. There are also mountains, deserts, rainforests, lakes and lots of other amazing places for you to explore.

Grand Canyon
Take a peek over the edge of the gigantic Grand Canyon – it's a very long way down.

Hawai'i
Watch volcanoes erupt in Hawai'i. There are fireworks all year round.

Seals

Atlantic cod

Baffin Bay

Polar bears

Beavers

Hudson Bay

Moose

Grizzly bears

Grey

Arctic Ocean

Mackenzie River

Bison

Denali (Mt McKinley)

Volcanoes

Hibiscus

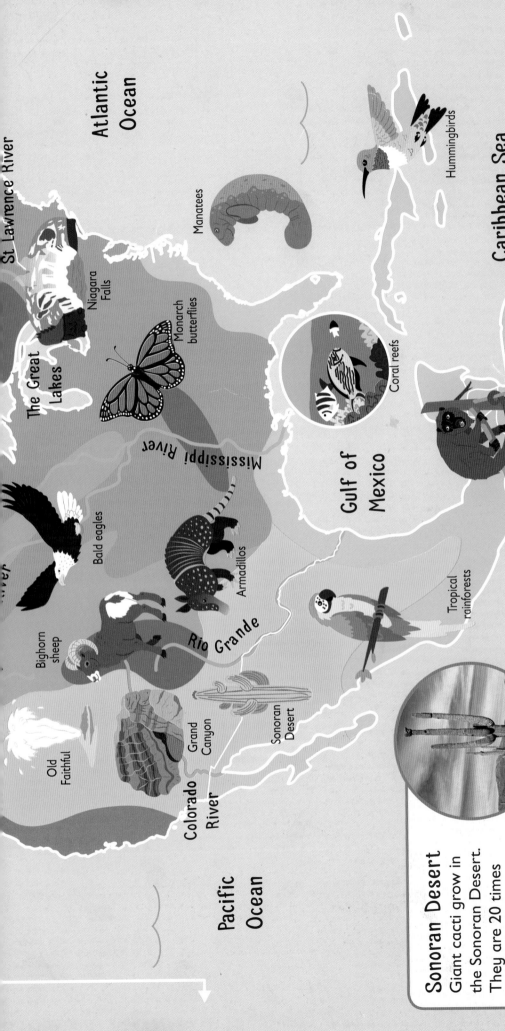

Atlantic
Ocean

St Lawrence River

The Great
Lakes

Niagara
Falls

Manatees

Hummingbirds

Caribbean Sea

Monarch
butterflies

Mississippi River

Bald eagles

Coral reefs

Armadillos

Gulf of
Mexico

Howler
monkeys

Bighorn
sheep

Rio Grande

Tropical
rainforests

Old
Faithful

Colorado
River

Grand
Canyon

Sonoran
Desert

Pacific
Ocean

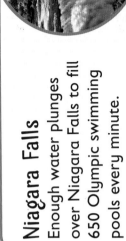

Niagara Falls
Enough water plunges over Niagara Falls to fill 650 Olympic swimming pools every minute.

Sonoran Desert
Giant cacti grow in the Sonoran Desert. They are 20 times taller than you.

FAST FACTS

Size: 24.5 million sq km
Population: 565 million people
Number of countries: 23
Biggest country: Canada

Highest mountain: Denali, USA
Biggest splash: Niagara Falls
Windiest place: Tornado Alley
Tallest tree: Coast redwood
Longest caves: Mammoth Caves

CANADA AND THE FAR NORTH

Canada is a huge country in North America. Bordering the Pacific, Atlantic and Arctic Oceans, it has the longest coastline in the world. On land, Canada borders the USA in the south.

Arctic Ocean

Oil

Polar bears

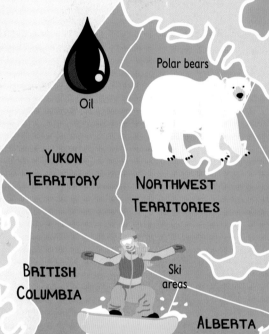

YUKON TERRITORY

NORTHWEST TERRITORIES

NUNAVUT

BRITISH COLUMBIA

Ski areas

Mounted police

Pacific Ocean

Hudson Bay

ALBERTA

MANITOBA

Totem poles

Calgary Stampede

SASKATCHEWAN

Edmonton

Calgary

Vancouver

Canadian-Pacific Railroad

CANADA

Timber industry

Winnipeg

Poutine
Feeling hungry? Stop in Montréal for a bowl of poutine – chips, topped with cheese curds and gravy.

Sawmill
Work a shift at a sawmill where timber from Canada's forests is cut into planks of wood.

10

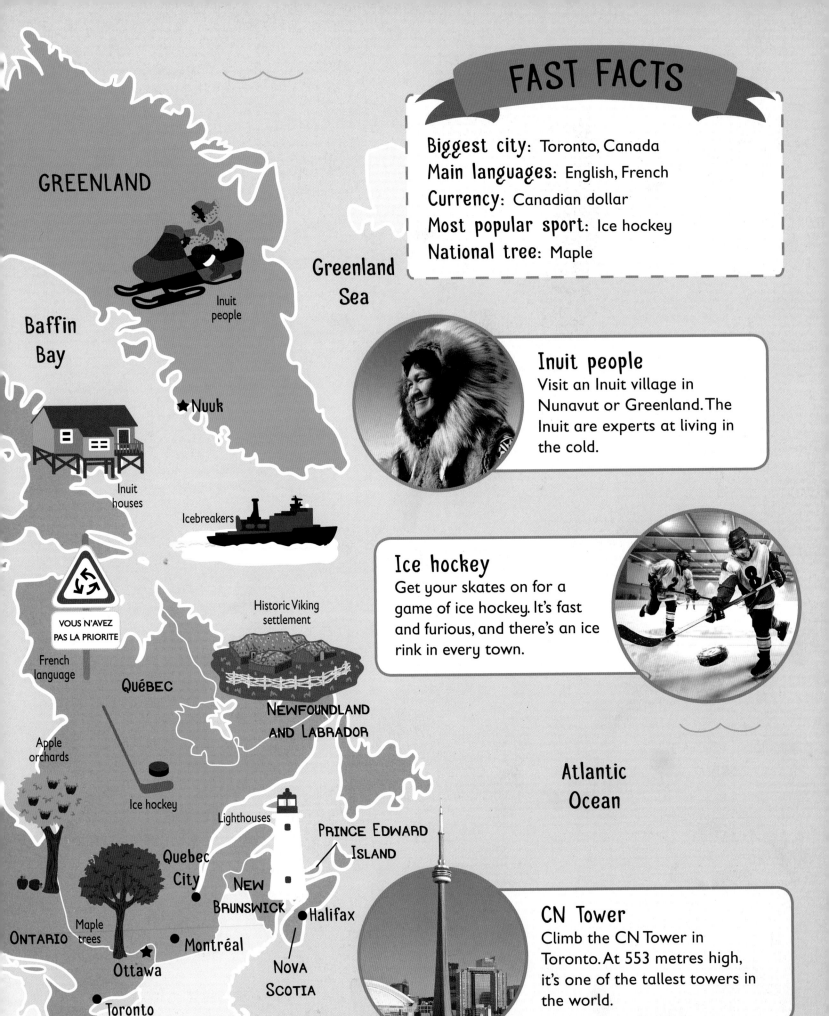

GREENLAND

Baffin
Bay

Greenland
Sea

Inuit
people

Nuuk

Inuit
houses

Icebreakers

French
language

QUÉBEC

Historic Viking
settlement

NEWFOUNDLAND
AND LABRADOR

Apple
orchards

Ice hockey

Lighthouses

PRINCE EDWARD
ISLAND

Quebec
City

NEW
BRUNSWICK

Halifax

Maple
trees

ONTARIO

Montréal

Ottawa

NOVA
SCOTIA

Toronto

Atlantic
Ocean

FAST FACTS

Biggest city: Toronto, Canada
Main languages: English, French
Currency: Canadian dollar
Most popular sport: Ice hockey
National tree: Maple

Inuit people
Visit an Inuit village in
Nunavut or Greenland. The
Inuit are experts at living in
the cold.

Ice hockey
Get your skates on for a
game of ice hockey. It's fast
and furious, and there's an ice
rink in every town.

CN Tower
Climb the CN Tower in
Toronto. At 553 metres high,
it's one of the tallest towers in
the world.

ALASKA

Gold

WASHINGTON

OREGON

Space Needle

MONTANA

NORTH DAKOTA

Wheat

Diamond mines

Golden Gate Bridge

HAWAI'I

Surfing

Pacific Ocean

NEVADA

CALIFORNIA

Wine country

Las Vegas

WELCOME TO Fabulous LAS VEGAS NEVADA

Technology

IDAHO

WYOMING

Coal mines

UTAH

Colorado River

SOUTH DAKOTA

Mt Rushmore

Missouri River

NEBRASKA

Corn

COLORADO

KANSAS

Baseball

ARIZONA

Rio Grande

NEW MEXICO

Oil

OKLAHOMA

Farming

TEXAS

Burger and fries

Baseball

Cheer on the players at a baseball game – it's one of the most popular sports in the USA.

THE USA

The USA (United States of America) is a rich and powerful country in North America. It is made up of 50 smaller states. The capital city of the USA is Washington D.C.

Hollywood

Spot a film star in Hollywood, California. Hundreds of films are made here every year.

Mount Rushmore
Come face-to-face with four great U.S. presidents, carved into the mountian. Each head is **18** metres tall.

Statue of Liberty
Take a boat trip around New York harbour to see the famous Statue of Liberty.

Ice Hockey

MICHIGAN

NEW HAMPSHIRE

VERMONT

MAINE

WISCONSIN

Car industry

Statue of Liberty

MASSACHUSETTS

MINNESOTA

NEW YORK

RHODE ISLAND

CONNECTICUT

IOWA

PENNSYLVANIA

NEW JERSEY

ILLINOIS

Car racing

INDIANA

OHIO

DELAWARE

MARYLAND

WEST VIRGINIA

White House

Washington D.C.

MISSOURI

KENTUCKY

VIRGINIA

Mississippi River

ARKANSAS

TENNESSEE

NORTH CAROLINA

SOUTH CAROLINA

American football

ALABAMA

GEORGIA

Space Centre

LOUISIANA

MISSISSIPPI

FLORIDA

Atlantic Ocean

White House

Visit the White House in Washington D.C. It's where the President of the USA lives.

Gulf of Mexico

Snorkeling

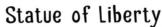

FAST FACTS

Biggest city: New York City

Tallest skyscraper: One World Trade Center, New York City

Smallest state: Rhode Island

Busiest airport: Atlanta

Most famous food: Hot dogs, hamburgers

MEXICO AND CENTRAL AMERICA

Mexico and Central America form a bridge of land that links North and South America. In this region, you'll find steamy jungles, ancient ruins, sandy beaches, volcanic islands and bustling cities.

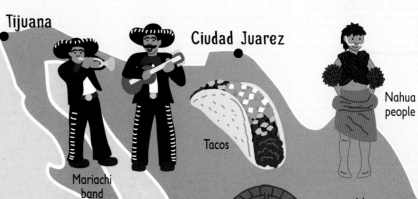

Tijuana

Ciudad Juarez

Mariachi band

Tacos

Nahua people

Monterrey

Aztec Sun Stone

Corn

Guadalajara

MEXICO

Mexico City

Puebla

Chilli peppers

Cliff divers

Mexico City
Snap photos of the ancient Aztec ruins in Mexico City. It's one of the biggest cities in the world.

Day of the Dead
Buy a spooky sugar skull for the Day of the Dead festival and dress up as a skeleton.

GUATEMALA

Pacific Ocean

FAST FACTS

Biggest city: Mexico City, Mexico
Tallest mountain: Pico de Orizaba, Mexico
Main language: Spanish
Favourite sport: Football
Popular food: Tortillas, tacos

Cuban dance

Dance the mambo in Cuba. It's quick and catchy, and you won't be able to keep your feet still.

Caribbean beaches

For a relaxing holiday, head to the sunny islands of the West Indies in the Caribbean Sea.

Oil rigs
Drill for oil in the Gulf of Mexico. Oil rigs there produce 3 billion barrels of oil each day.

Panama Canal
Take a cruise along the busy Panama Canal. It links the Atlantic and Pacific Oceans.

Atlantic Ocean

Gulf of Mexico

THE BAHAMAS

CUBA

Havana

JAMAICA

Kingston

HAITI

Port-au-Prince

DOMINICAN REPUBLIC

Santo Domingo

PUERTO RICO

ANGUILLA

Baseball

GUADELOUPE

DOMINICA

MARTINIQUE

SAINT LUCIA

BARBADOS

TRINIDAD AND TOBAGO

Cricket

Caribbean Sea

BELIZE

HONDURAS

Bananas

Mayan Pyramids

Guatemala City Cathedral

Guatemala City

Belmopan

Tegucigalpa

San Salvador

EL SALVADOR

NICARAGUA

Managua

San José

COSTA RICA

Tropical rainforests

PANAMA

PANAMA CANAL

Panama City

SOUTH AMERICA

A long chain of mountains, called the Andes, runs along the continent of South America. On the western side of the mountains, you'll find the bone-dry Atacama Desert. On the eastern side is the biggest rainforest on Earth.

Angel Falls
Angel Falls plunges 980 metres off a mountain. It's the world's highest waterfall.

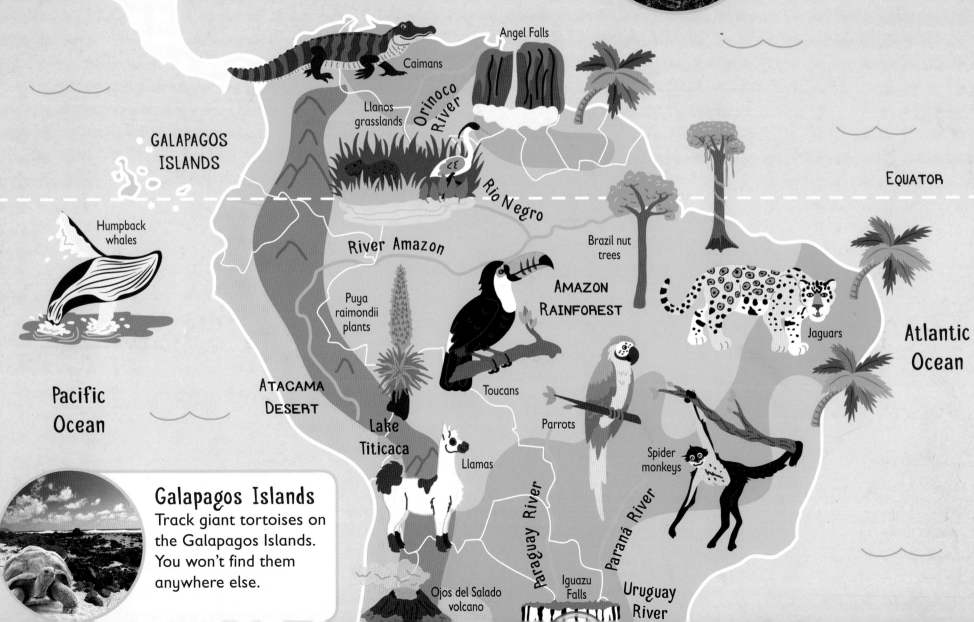

Caimans

Angel Falls

Llanos grasslands

Orinoco River

GALAPAGOS ISLANDS

Rio Negro

EQUATOR

Humpback whales

River Amazon

Brazil nut trees

Puya raimondii plants

AMAZON RAINFOREST

Jaguars

Atlantic Ocean

Pacific Ocean

ATACAMA DESERT

Toucans

Parrots

Spider monkeys

Lake Titicaca

Llamas

Galapagos Islands
Track giant tortoises on the Galapagos Islands. You won't find them anywhere else.

Paraguay River

Paraná River

Uruguay River

Ojos del Salado volcano

Iguazu Falls

Green sea turtles

Chinchillas

Mt Aconcagua

ANDES MOUNTAINS

Pampas grass

Periot Moreno glacier

Tierra del Fuego

Penguins

Amazon rainforest

Marvel at the world's biggest rainforest. It grows along the banks of the River Amazon.

Andes Mountains

Take a trek through the snow-capped Andes – the longest mountain range in the world.

Perito Moreno glacier

Go glacier spotting in southern Argentina. It's very cold, so you'll need to wrap up nice and warm!

FAST FACTS

Size: 17.8 million sq km
Population: 423 million people
Number of countries: 12
Biggest country: Brazil

Biggest volcano: Ojos del Salado
Highest lake: Lake Titicaca
Longest river: Amazon
Driest desert: Atacama
Thinnest country: Chile

WESTERN SOUTH AMERICA

The western part of South America stretches along the Andes Mountains. It includes the countries of Venezuela, Colombia, Ecuador, Peru, Bolivia and Chile.

Atlantic Ocean

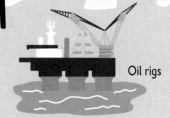
Cumbia dance

Oil rigs

Caracas

VENEZUELA

Chilli peppers

Bolivar

Bogota

COLOMBIA

GALAPAGOS ISLANDS

Corn

EQUATOR

Quito

ECUADOR

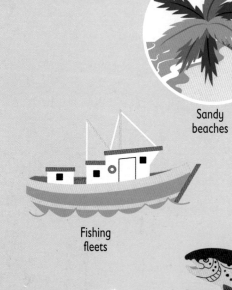
Sandy beaches

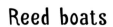
Coffee

Reed boats
Learn how to make a reed boat on Lake Titicaca. The reeds grow all around the lake.

Inti Raymi Festival

Fishing fleets

Lima

PERU

Peanuts

BOLIVIA

Brown trout

Nazca Lines

Lake Titicaca

La Paz

Woven Blankets

Pastel de choclo

Pan-American Highway

Take a drive along the Pan-American Highway. It stretches right along the west coast.

Antarctic research vessels

Football

FAST FACTS

Highest capital city: La Paz, Bolivia

Most southerly point: Cape Horn, Chile

Main language: Spanish

Biggest city: Lima, Peru

Most precious resources: Oil, emeralds

Quechua people

Help the Quechua people of Peru to look after their llamas. They use their wool to make clothes.

CHILE

Copper mines

Pacific Ocean

Santiago

Space observatories

Pastel de choclo

Tuck into a slice of pastel de choclo, a pie from Chile. It's made from meat topped with sweetcorn.

Machu Picchu

Climb to the ancient Inca city of Machu Picchu in Peru. It's high up in the Andes Mountains.

EASTERN SOUTH AMERICA

The eastern part of South America includes Brazil, the biggest country and French Guiana, the smallest country. There are also many big cities, such as Sao Paulo and Buenos Aires.

Brasília Cathedral
Visit the stunning Roman Catholic cathedral in Brasília. It is mostly made from glass.

Yanomami
Spend time with the Yanomami people. They have lived in the rainforest for centuries.

SURINAME

Guiana Space Centre

Georgetown

Paramaribo

Cayenne

GUYANA

FRENCH GUIANA

EQUATOR

Coffee plantations

River Amazon

Oranges

Brazil nuts

Bananas

Feijoada

Cattle

BRAZIL

Christ the Redeemer statue

Brasília

Rio Carnival
Dress up in your most colourful clothes and join the dancers at the Carnival in Rio de Janeiro.

Paraguay River

Paraná River

PARAGUAY

Christ the Redeemer
Still in Rio, take a snap of the huge statue of Jesus that stands on top of a nearby hill.

Elephant seals

Pato

Mountain climbing

FAST FACTS

Biggest city: Sao Paulo, Brazil
Most popular sport: Football
Best beach: Copacabana
Most valuable crops: Bananas, coffee
Main language: Portuguese (Brazil)

Banana plantations

Gaucho ride
Ride with gauchos (cowboys) on the pampas in Argentina as they round up their herds of cattle.

ARGENTINA

Buenos Aires

Montevideo

URUGUAY

Diamonds

Mate tea

Atlantic Ocean

Surfing

Itaipu Dam

Uruguay River

Football

Ceibo flowers

Sao Paulo

Rio de Janeiro

Pacific Ocean

AFRICA

Africa is a huge continent, almost completely surrounded by sea. It has scorching deserts, steamy rainforests, rolling grasslands and snow-capped mountains. Africa is famous for its amazing animals – look out for zebras, elephants and gorillas, to name just a few.

River Nile
Take a sightseeing boat trip along the Nile. At 6,650 kilometres, it is the world's longest river.

Sahara Desert
Take a camel ride across the Sahara – it's the biggest and sandiest desert on Earth.

FAST FACTS

Size: 30.22 million square kilometres
Population: 1.2 billion
Number of countries: 55
Biggest country: Algeria

Highest mountain: Mount Kilimanjaro
Deepest valley: Great Rift Valley
Largest desert: Sahara Desert
Longest river: River Nile
Fastest animal: Cheetah

Cape Verde Islands

Mediterranean Sea

Atlas Mountains

Coral reefs

Date palms

Jerboas

River Nile

Oases

Locusts

Camels

SAHARA DESERT

Oryx

Red Sea

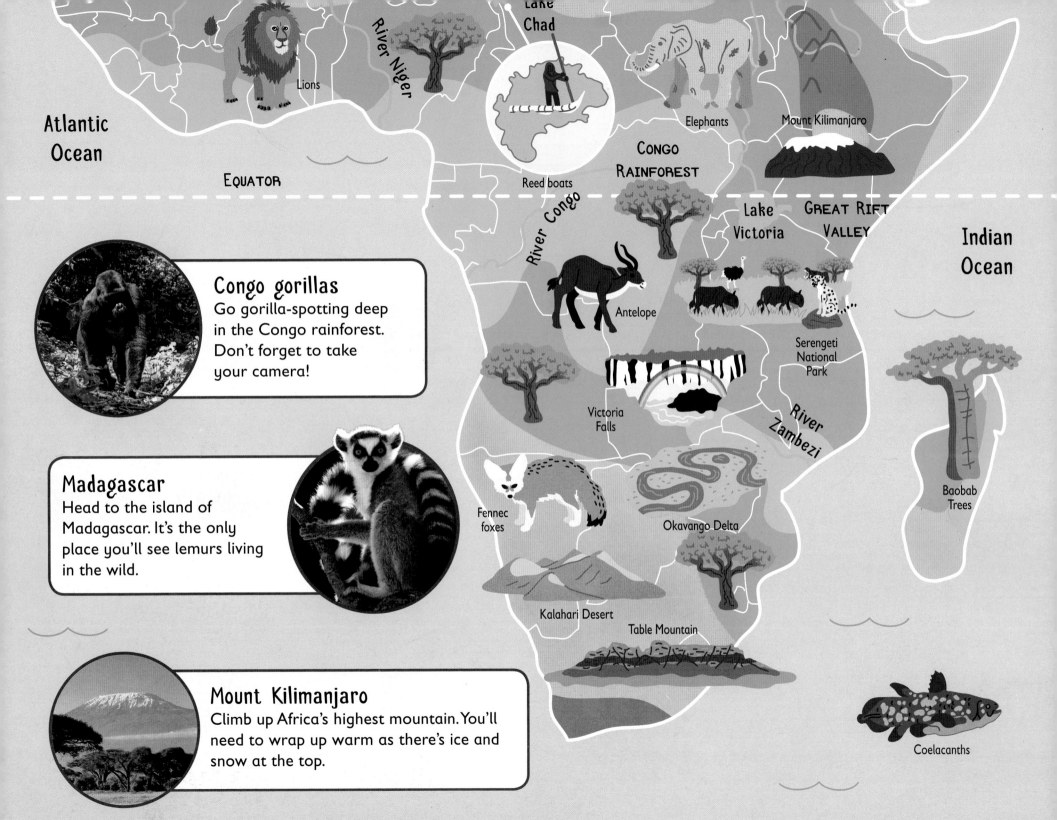

Atlantic Ocean

EQUATOR

Lions

River Niger

Lake Chad

Reed boats

Elephants

CONGO RAINFOREST

Mount Kilimanjaro

River Congo

Lake Victoria

GREAT RIFT VALLEY

Indian Ocean

Antelope

Serengeti National Park

Victoria Falls

River Zambezi

Baobab Trees

Fennec foxes

Okavango Delta

Kalahari Desert

Table Mountain

Coelacanths

Congo gorillas
Go gorilla-spotting deep in the Congo rainforest. Don't forget to take your camera!

Madagascar
Head to the island of Madagascar. It's the only place you'll see lemurs living in the wild.

Mount Kilimanjaro
Climb up Africa's highest mountain. You'll need to wrap up warm as there's ice and snow at the top.

NORTHERN AFRICA

Northern Africa is made up of the countries in and around the Sahara Desert. One of these countries — Egypt — is famous for being the home of the ancient Egyptians who built the pyramids.

Mediterranean Sea

★ Tunis — TUNISIA

★ Tripoli — LIBYA

Leptis Magna

Camels

Date palms

Lake Chad

★ N'Djamena — CHAD

Fulani people

NIGER

Couscous

★ Algiers — ALGERIA

Berber people

Football

★ Niamey

Sheep

★ Rabat — MOROCCO

Tagines

Sugar beets

Timbuktu

Niger River

MALI

★ Bamako

Sandy beaches

Folk music

MAURITANIA

★ Laayoune — WESTERN SAHARA

★ Nouakchott

Atlantic Ocean

Fishing boats

Dogon dance

Take part in a traditional Dogon dance in Mali. You stand on stilts to imitate a long-legged bird.

FAST FACTS

Biggest city: Cairo, Egypt
Longest canal: Suez Canal, Egypt
Hottest place: Al'Aziziyah, Libya
Most widely spoken language: Arabic
Most useful plant: Date palm

Pyramids

Take a trip back in time to the pyramids in Egypt. They were built thousands of years ago.

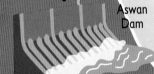

Oil rigs

Suez Canal

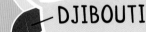

Tuareg

Ride a camel with Tuareg traders. Don't forget to cover your face with a scarf to keep out the desert sand!

Cairo ★

Pyramids

River Nile

EGYPT

Traditional djellaba robes

Aswan Dam

Great Mosque of Kairouan

Visit this ancient mosque in Tunisia to learn about Islam, the religion followed by many North Africans.

SUDAN

Red Sea

Cotton

Khartoum ★   Spices

★ Asmara

— **ERITREA**

Dinka people

ETHIOPIA   — **DJIBOUTI**

Addis Ababa ★

Oranges

Coffee beans

Indian Ocean

Desert oasis

Rest at a desert oasis where water springs up from underground so that plants can grow.

Equator

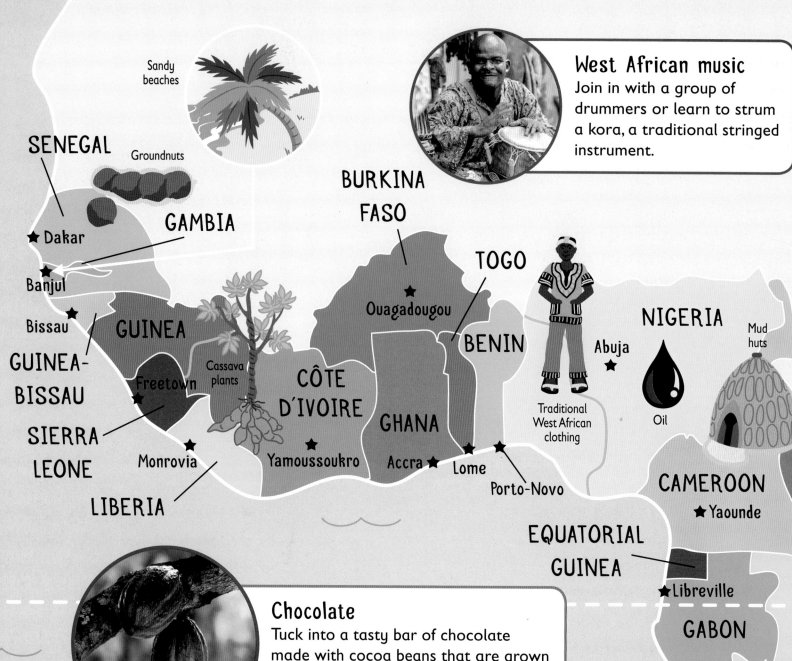

Sandy beaches

Groundnuts

West African music
Join in with a group of drummers or learn to strum a kora, a traditional stringed instrument.

SENEGAL

GAMBIA

BURKINA FASO

TOGO

★ Dakar

★ Banjul

Bissau

GUINEA

GUINEA-BISSAU

SIERRA LEONE

Freetown

Cassava plants

CÔTE D'IVOIRE

Ouagadougou

BENIN

NIGERIA

Abuja ★

Oil

Mud huts

Traditional West African clothing

GHANA

Monrovia

Yamoussoukro

Accra ★ Lome

Porto-Novo

LIBERIA

CAMEROON

★ Yaounde

EQUATORIAL GUINEA

★ Libreville

Chocolate
Tuck into a tasty bar of chocolate made with cocoa beans that are grown in west Africa.

GABON

Brazzaville

Kinshasa

Atlantic Ocean

REPUBLIC OF THE CONGO

FAST FACTS

Biggest city: Lagos, Nigeria
Most popular sport: Football
Biggest oil producer: Nigeria
Best place for fishing: Lake Victoria
Best beaches: Seychelles

Nollywood
Get to star in a 'Nollywood' film in Nigeria. Hundreds of films are made here each year.

WEST, CENTRAL AND EAST AFRICA

On your long journey across Africa, you'll travel from Senegal in the west to Kenya in the east. You'll pass through many amazing countries and meet many fascinating people.

Masai people

Meet the Masai people of east Africa. They travel across the land with their herds of cattle.

CENTRAL AFRICAN REPUBLIC

Basketball

Lions

SOUTH SUDAN

★ Juba

Cattle

Laas Geel cave paintings

angui

★

DEMOCRATIC REPUBLIC OF THE CONGO

UGANDA

Kampala ★

Mogadishu ★

SOMALIA

EQUATOR

Mbuti people

RWANDA

Lake Victoria

Mt Nyiragongo

★ Kigali

Nairobi ★

KENYA

SEYCHELLES

Victoria ★

Bujumbura ★

BURUNDI

Tourists on safari

Indian Ocean

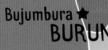

★ Dodoma

Diamonds

Masks

TANZANIA

Spice markets

Ancient people

Head for Olduvai Gorge in Tanzania, where bones from the earliest humans were found.

SOUTHERN AFRICA

The southern part of Africa has big cities, beautiful scenery and a long coastline with the Atlantic and Indian Oceans. The biggest country in the region is South Africa.

Safari adventure
Spot lions, giraffes, zebras and hippos in Botswana's beautiful savannah.

Diamond mine
Dig for diamonds in Angola. The country has some of the world's biggest diamond mines.

Skeleton Coast
Look out for ghostly shipwrecks. Thousands of ships have run aground along this coast of Namibia.

Bunny chow
Try a plate of bunny chow in South Africa. It's a loaf of bread filled with spicy curry.

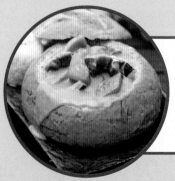

Atlantic Ocean

SKELETON COAST

★ Luanda

ANGOLA

Oil

Diamonds

Traditional huts

Cricket

Haru oms

BOTSWANA

NAMIBIA

★ Windhoek

Himba people

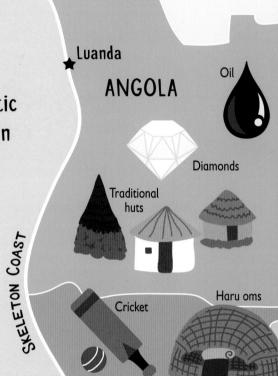

Surfing

Gold mining

Cape Town ★

CAPE AGULHAS

Fishing trip
Go fishing on Lake Malawi. There are more than 1,000 different kinds of fish to catch.

Baobab trees
Try to reach your arms round the massive trunk of a Baobab tree on Madagascar. Baobabs store water in their trunk so they still have plenty during times of drought.

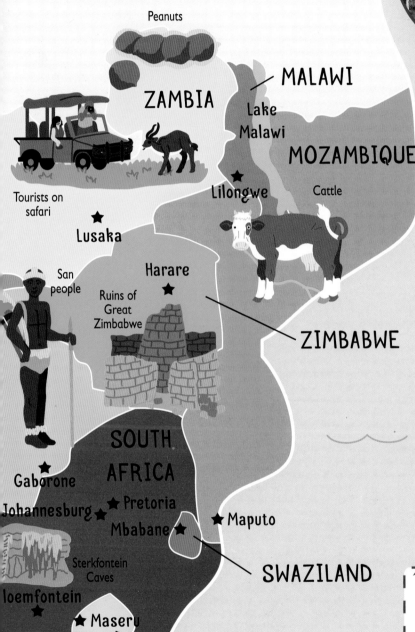

Peanuts

ZAMBIA

MALAWI

Lake Malawi

MOZAMBIQUE

Tourists on safari

Lilongwe

Cattle

Lusaka

San people

Harare

Ruins of Great Zimbabwe

ZIMBABWE

SOUTH AFRICA

Gaborone

Johannesburg

Pretoria

Maputo

Mbabane

SWAZILAND

Sterkfontein Caves

loemfontein

Maseru

LESOTHO

Rooibos tea

Lemurs

Antananarivo

MADAGASCAR

Baobab trees

FAST FACTS

Most southerly point: Cape Agulhas

Biggest city: Cape Town, South Africa

Top sports: Football and cricket

Most valuable resources: Gold and diamonds

Biggest shopping mall: Gateway Theatre of Shopping (Durban, South Africa)

EUROPE

By size, Europe is the second-smallest continent, but it is the third biggest by population. Only Asia and Africa have more people living there. Europe reaches from the Atlantic Ocean in the west across to Asia in the east.

Fjords
Take a cruise along the Norwegian fjords. They're long, thin valleys carved out by glaciers.

Volcanoes

Iceland
Iceland is an island in the North Atlantic Ocean, famous for volcanoes, geysers and glaciers.

Atlantic Ocean

North Sea

Atlantic cod

Red deer

River Thames

Mt Etna
Climb fiery Mt Etna on the island of Sicily. It's one of the world's most active volcanoes.

River Rhône

PYRENEES

Spanish lynx

FAST FACTS

Size: 9.9 million square kilometres

Population: 740 million

Number of countries: 47

Biggest country: Russia

Highest mountain: Mt Elbrus, Russia

Longest river: River Volga

Largest lake: Lake Ladoga

Highest active volcano: Mt Etna, Italy

Rarest animal: Spanish lynx

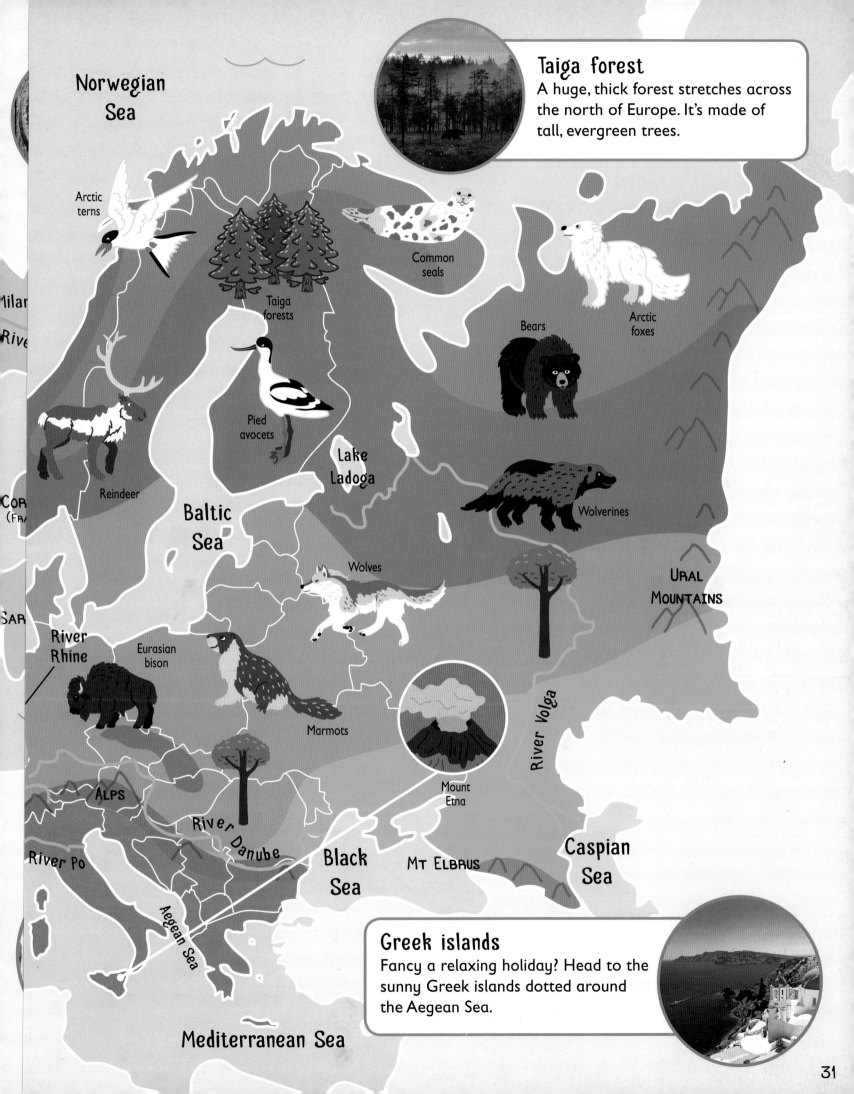

Norwegian Sea

Taiga forest
A huge, thick forest stretches across the north of Europe. It's made of tall, evergreen trees.

Milan

River

Arctic terns

Taiga forests

Common seals

Bears

Arctic foxes

Pied avocets

Lake Ladoga

Reindeer

COR
(FRA

Baltic Sea

Wolverines

SAR

Wolves

URAL MOUNTAINS

River Rhine

Eurasian bison

Marmots

Mount Etna

River Volga

ALPS

River Po

River Danube

Black Sea

MT ELBRUS

Caspian Sea

Aegean Sea

Greek islands
Fancy a relaxing holiday? Head to the sunny Greek islands dotted around the Aegean Sea.

Mediterranean Sea

WESTERN EUROPE

Western Europe stretches from France in the west to Austria in the east. It includes the two large countries of France and Germany, and many smaller countries around them.

Eiffel Tower
Climb almost 300 metres to the top of the Eiffel Tower for a spectacular view of Paris.

Cheese-making
Try making some cheese in the Netherlands. The most popular kinds are Edam and Gouda.

BELGIUM —

Channel Tunnel

Paris

Winter sports
Spend the winter skiing or snowboarding in the Alps mountains. They're a brilliant place for winter sports.

Standing stones

FRANCE

River Loire

• Nantes

Tour de France
Take part in the world's greatest bike race. You'll cycle around 3,500 kilometres in three weeks.

Atlantic Ocean

Bordeaux

Cave paintings

FAST FACTS

Biggest country (by area): France
Smallest country: Liechtenstein
Longest bike race: Tour de France
Best chocolate: Belgium, Switzerland
Most crowded city: Berlin

Historic chateaux

Toulous

ANDORRA —

Andorra la Vella ★

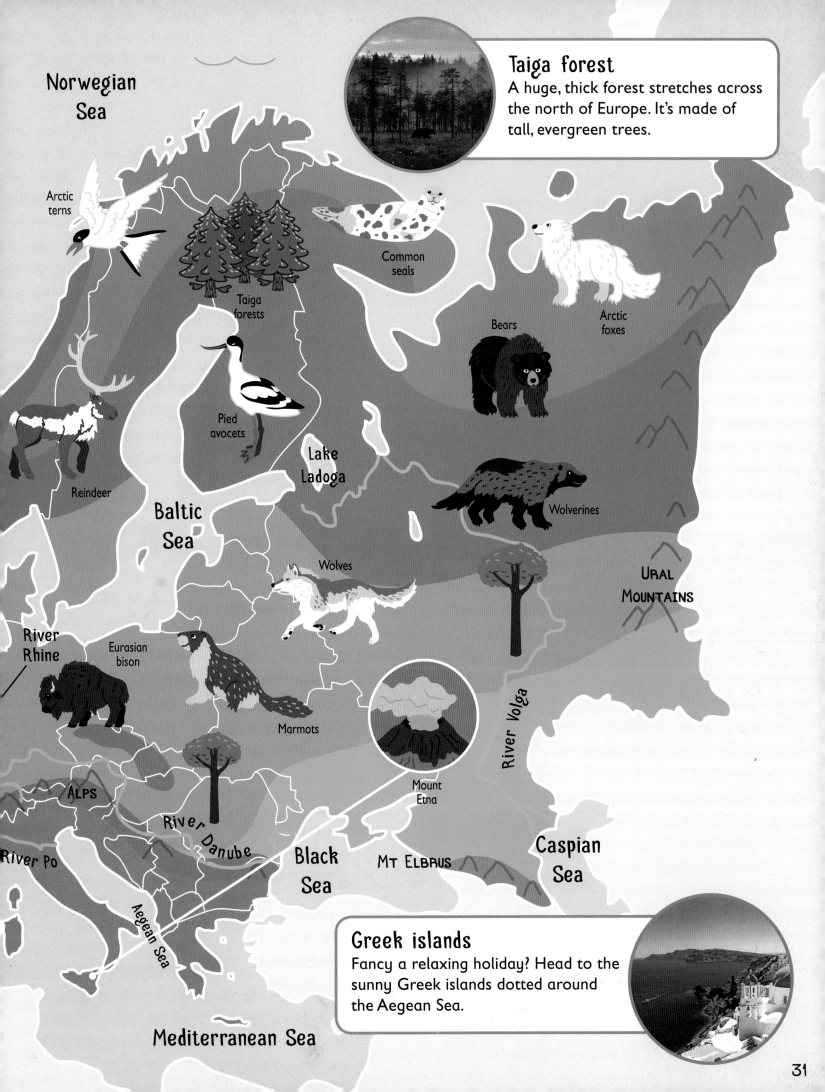

Norwegian Sea

Arctic terns

Taiga forest
A huge, thick forest stretches across the north of Europe. It's made of tall, evergreen trees.

Taiga forests

Common seals

Bears

Arctic foxes

Pied avocets

Reindeer

Lake Ladoga

Baltic Sea

Wolverines

Wolves

URAL MOUNTAINS

River Rhine

Eurasian bison

Marmots

Mount Etna

River Volga

ALPS

River Danube

Black Sea

MT ELBRUS

Caspian Sea

River Po

Aegean Sea

Greek islands
Fancy a relaxing holiday? Head to the sunny Greek islands dotted around the Aegean Sea.

Mediterranean Sea

31

SOUTHERN EUROPE

The countries of southern Europe lie around the Mediterranean Sea. They have warm, sunny weather which makes many of them popular places to go on holiday.

Gondolas
Go on a gondola ride through the canals of Venice, a beautiful and historic city built on dozens of man-made islands.

Atlantic Ocean

Port

Porto

Guggenheim Museum

Cork Trees

Madrid

Oranges

Sagrada Familia Cathedral

Barcelona

SPAIN

Valencia

MENORCA

MALLORCA

IBIZA

Lisbon

Olive trees

Paella

PORTUGAL

Seville

Fishing

Flamenco
Get your dancing shoes on for some flamenco. It's a fast and furious dance from Spain.

FAST FACTS

Biggest country: Spain
Smallest country: Vatican City
Top holiday spot: Mallorca
Most fiestas (festivals): Spain
Best ice cream: Italy

Pizza time
Tuck into a delicious pizza. Along with pasta and ice cream, it's Italy's most famous food.

Vatican City
See the Vatican City in Rome. It's home to the Pope, head of the Roman Catholic Church.

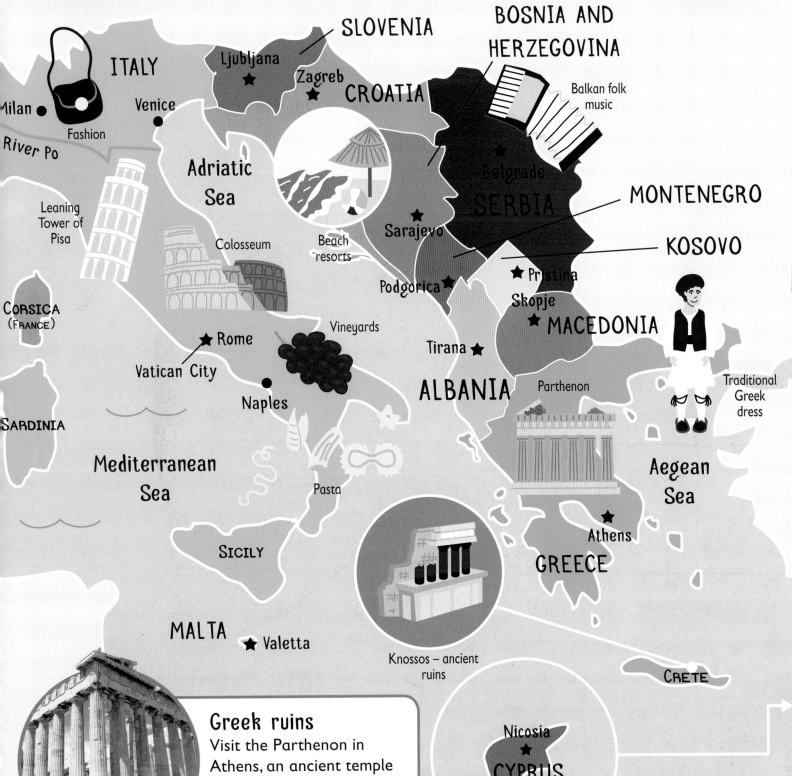

SLOVENIA

BOSNIA AND HERZEGOVINA

ITALY

Ljubljana

Zagreb

CROATIA

Balkan folk music

Milan

Venice

Fashion

River Po

Adriatic Sea

Belgrade

SERBIA

MONTENEGRO

Leaning Tower of Pisa

Colosseum

Beach resorts

Sarajevo

KOSOVO

Pristina

CORSICA (FRANCE)

Podgorica

Skopje

Vineyards

MACEDONIA

Rome

Vatican City

Tirana

Traditional Greek dress

SARDINIA

Naples

ALBANIA

Parthenon

Mediterranean Sea

Aegean Sea

Pasta

SICILY

Athens

GREECE

Knossos – ancient ruins

MALTA

Valetta

CRETE

Greek ruins
Visit the Parthenon in Athens, an ancient temple that was built almost 2,500 years ago.

Nicosia

CYPRUS

WESTERN EUROPE

Western Europe stretches from France in the west to Austria in the east. It includes the two large countries of France and Germany, and many smaller countries around them.

North Sea

Eiffel Tower
Climb almost 300 metres to the top of the Eiffel Tower for a spectacular view of Paris.

Cheese-making
Try making some cheese in the Netherlands. The most popular kinds are Edam and Gouda.

BELGIUM —

Channel Tunnel

Paris ★

Winter sports
Spend the winter skiing or snowboarding in the Alps mountains. They're a brilliant place for winter sports.

Standing stones

FRANCE

River Loire

Tour de France
Take part in the world's greatest bike race. You'll cycle around 3,500 kilometres in three weeks.

● Nantes

Atlantic Ocean

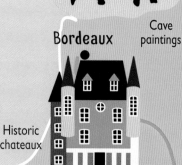

Bordeaux ●

Cave paintings

FAST FACTS

Historic chateaux

Biggest country (by area): France
Smallest country: Liechtenstein
Longest bike race: Tour de France
Best chocolate: Belgium, Switzerland
Most crowded city: Berlin

Toulouse ●

ANDORRA —

Andorra la Vella ★

THE NETHERLANDS

Baltic Sea

Atomium

Hamburg

Brandenburg Gate

River Elbe

Amsterdam ★

Berlin ★

Windmills and tulips

Football

Currywurst

Rotterdam

● Antwerp

Cologne Cathedral

GERMANY

ussels ★

Waffles

Super sausages
Sausages are very popular in Germany. There are lots of different kinds, such as bratwurst and currywurst.

Luxembourg City

LUXEMBOURG

Frankfurt

Oktoberfest

Bread and cheese

Hiking

River Seine

Vineyards

River Rhine

● Munich

Vienna

Skiing

Bern ★ Zurich

Vad

SWITZERLAND

Geneva

Lyon ●

LIECHTENSTEIN

River Rhône

Swiss chocolate

Lavender fields

Perfume

Neuschwanstein Castle
This fabulous fairytale castle perches on a mountaintop in Bavaria. It was built in 1869.

● Nice

Marseilles

Mediterranean Sea

CORSICA

35

NORTHERN EUROPE

The northern part of Europe has colder weather than the rest of the continent. The middle of Iceland is covered in a thick sheet of ice. Norway, Sweden, Finland and Denmark are called Scandinavia.

Reindeer herding
Herd reindeer with the Sami people who live in the freezing far north of Scandinavia.

ICELAND

Geysers

Sheep

Reykjavik

Atlantic Ocean

Royal family
Queen Elizabeth II lives in Buckingham Palace, London. She is head of the British Royal Family.

Loch Ness Monster
If you dare, go monster spotting in Loch Ness, Scotland. No one knows if it's real, or not.

FAST FACTS

Biggest country (by area): Sweden
Smallest country: Denmark
Biggest city: London, United Kingdom
Coldest city: Reykjavik, Iceland
Biggest museum: British Museum, London

UNITED KINGDOM

Bagpipes

SCOTLAND

NORTHERN IRELAND

Edinburgh

North Sea

Fish and chips

IRELAND

Dublin

Manchester

Shamrocks

WALES

ENGLAND

Irish Sea

Londo

Stonehenge

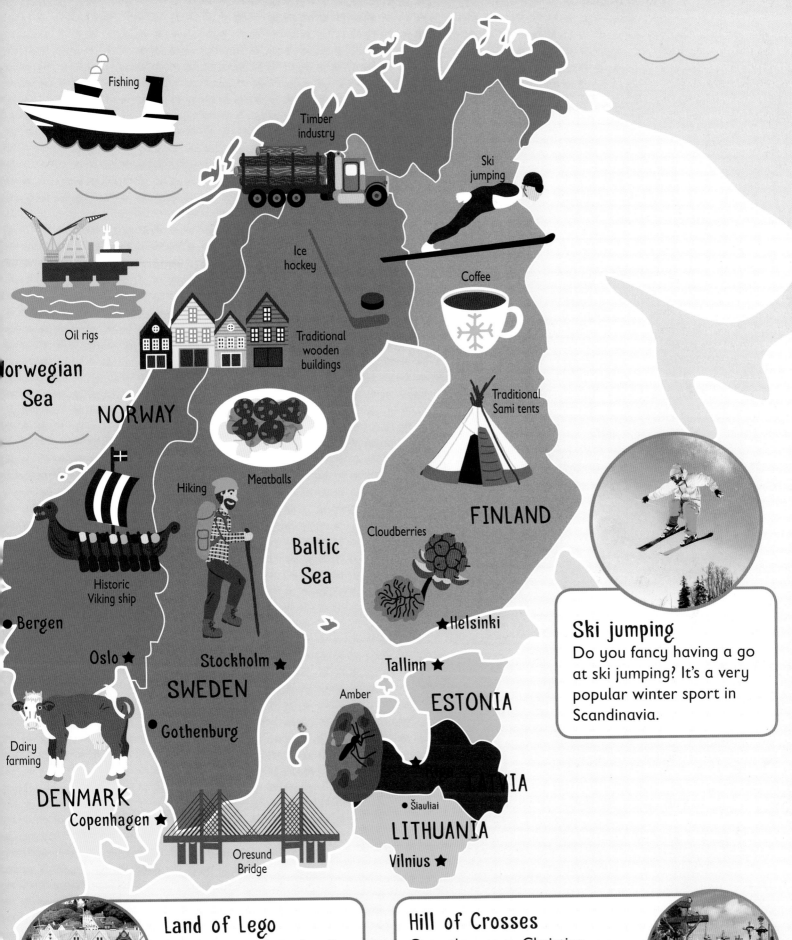

Fishing

Timber industry

Ski jumping

Ice hockey

Coffee

Oil rigs

Norwegian Sea

Traditional wooden buildings

Traditional Sami tents

NORWAY

Meatballs

Hiking

FINLAND

Cloudberries

Historic Viking ship

Baltic Sea

● Bergen

● Helsinki

Oslo ★

Stockholm ★

Tallinn ★

Amber

ESTONIA

SWEDEN

● Gothenburg

Dairy farming

Šiauliai

DENMARK

LITHUANIA

Copenhagen ★

Oresund Bridge

Vilnius ★

Ski jumping
Do you fancy having a go at ski jumping? It's a very popular winter sport in Scandinavia.

Land of Lego
Take a trip to Legoland® in Denmark. The buildings are made from millions of Lego® bricks.

Hill of Crosses
Over the years, Christian pilgrims have left thousands of crosses on this hill near Šiauliai in Lithuania.

Baltic Sea

Gdansk

Gingerbread

POLAND

BELARUS

Minsk

Mir Castle

Ice hockey

Dumplings

Sugar beets

★ Warsaw

Palace of Culture

Krakow

Traditional Ukrainian dress

St Sophia Cathedral

Prague

CZECH REPUBLIC

Brno

Spissky Hrad Castle

Wheat

★ Kiev

UKRAINE

River Dm

SLOVAKIA

Painted Easter eggs

Bratislava ★

Budapest ★

Hungarian Parliament

Sheep

MOLDOVA

Chişinau ★

HUNGARY

Cluj

Peles Castle

ROMANIA

Odessa

Timişoăra

Bran

Handball

★ Bucharest

River Danube

Goulash
Goulash is a dish from Hungary. It's made from meat, vegetables and spicy red pepper.

Gaida bagpipes

Sofia ★

Plovdiv

BULGARIA

Dracula's castle
Visit Count Dracula's spooky castle near Bran in Romania. Watch out for thirsty vampires!

Mediterranean Sea

38

EASTERN EUROPE

The countries of eastern Europe lie between the Baltic Sea and the Middle East. They have big, modern cities but there are also many traditional farms in the countryside.

Cossack dancing
Dance like a Cossack in Ukraine. It's very acrobatic with lots of jumps and spins.

Kharkiv

Cossack dancing

Donetsk

Rose Festival
Head to the Rose Festival in Bulgaria. The roses are picked for their sweet-smelling oil.

Swallow's Nest Castle

Rugby union

Puppet show
Watch a puppet show in Slovakia. Some of the puppets are more than a hundred years old.

Black Sea

GEORGIA ★ Tbilisi

Folk music

AZERBAIJAN   Baku

Yerevan

ARMENIA

Carpets

Caspian Sea

RUSSIA

Russia is the world's biggest country. It is so huge that it reaches across two continents – Europe and Asia. Most people live in big cities in the European part. Russia is so wide that it has 11 different time zones!

Bandy

Bandy is a popular sport, similar to ice hockey but played with a ball instead of a flat puck. It is sometimes called 'Russian hockey'.

Icebreakers

Barents Sea

Kara Sea

St Petersburg

Hermitage Museum

Borscht soup

Moscow

Kremlin

Nizhny Novgorod

Natural gas

Volga River

Dacha cottages

Perm

Oil

Nenets people

Yenisei River

Ob River

Volgograd

Yekaterinburg

Sochi

Caviar

Barley

Chelyabinsk

Irtysh River

Balalaika

Garlic

Omsk

St Basil's Cathedral

The onion domes of St Basil's Cathedral in Moscow look like the flames of a bonfire.

Novosibirsk

Wheat

Russian dolls

Russian dolls fit inside each other, getting smaller as they go. The dolls are made from wood.

Ballet show

Take your seat at the ballet – it's very popular in Russia. There are many famous ballet companies.

40

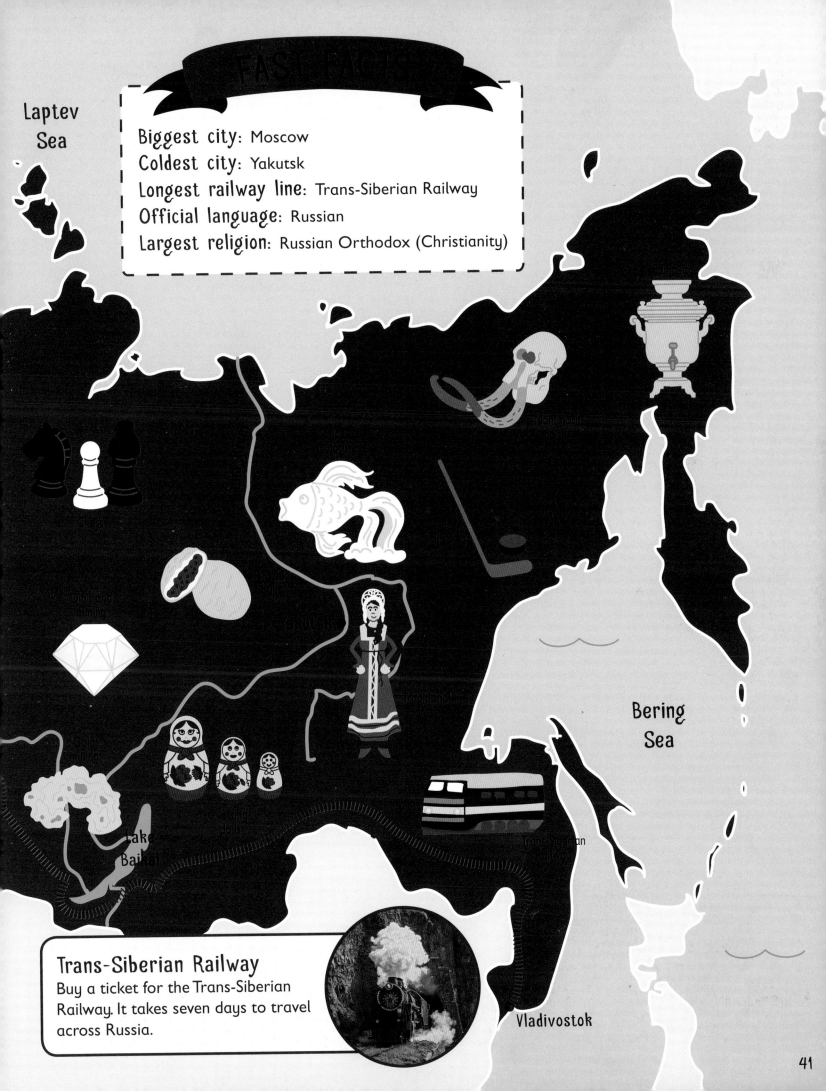

Laptev Sea

Biggest city: Moscow
Coldest city: Yakutsk
Longest railway line: Trans-Siberian Railway
Official language: Russian
Largest religion: Russian Orthodox (Christianity)

Bering Sea

Trans-Siberian Railway
Buy a ticket for the Trans-Siberian Railway. It takes seven days to travel across Russia.

Vladivostok

41

ASIA

Asia is the biggest continent. It covers almost a third of all the land on Earth. It also has more people than any other continent. In the north, Asia is cold and icy. In the south, it is hot and wet all year round.

Himalayas
The Himalayas to the north of India and Nepal are the highest mountain range in the world.

FAST FACTS

Size: 44.6 million square kilometres
Population: 4.4 billion people
Number of countries: 50
Biggest country: Russia
Smallest country: Maldives
Highest mountain: Mt Everest
Longest river: Yangtze River
Lowest point: Dead Sea
Biggest desert: Arabian Desert
Largest lake: Caspian Sea

Gobi Desert
Explore the huge Gobi Desert in China and Mongolia. Some people think that it's haunted.

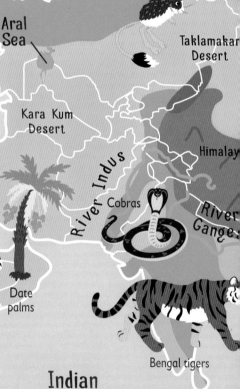

Bears

Ural Mountains

Jerboas

Aral Sea

Taklamakan Desert

Mt Ararat

Kara Kum Desert

River Tigris

River Indus

Himalay

Dead Sea

River Euphrates

Cobras

River Ganges

Arabian Desert

Date palms

Arabian oryx

Bengal tigers

Indian Ocean

Jellyfish

Narwhals

Lake Baikal
Amazing Lake Baikal is older, deeper and holds more fresh water than any other lake in the world.

Moose

Wolves

Seals

Taiga forests

Snow leopards

Lena River

Lake Baikal

Amur River

Kamchatka volcanoes

Yaks

Gobi Desert

Bactrian camels

Yellow River

Yangtze River

Mt Fuji

Mt Fuji
Stop off at cone-shaped Mt Fuji in Japan. People often climb it at night to watch the sun rise.

Pacific Ocean

Zhangjiajie National Forest Park

Rafflesia flowers

Orangutans

Rainforests

Coral reefs

Komodo dragons

Giant panda
Search for giant pandas in China. They live in mountain forests and mainly eat bamboo.

THE MIDDLE EAST

Most people in the Middle East are Muslims who follow the religion of Islam. More than half of the world's oil comes from the Middle East. It has made some countries very rich.

Blue Mosque

● Istanbul

Ankara

Ancient Greek city of Ephesus

Mediterranean Sea

LEBANON —

Jerusalem —

ISRAEL —

JORDAN —

Bazaars
Shop for spices, fabrics, jewellery and much more at one of the traditional marketplaces in the cities of the Middle East.

Dead Sea
Take a dip in the Dead Sea. It's so salty that you float in the water, and nothing can live in the lake.

Makkah
Makkah in Saudi Arabia is the holiest place for Muslims. They try to visit it at least once in their lives.

FAST FACTS

Biggest country: Saudi Arabia
Biggest city: Istanbul
Most spoken language: Arabic
Most precious resources: Oil and gas
Tallest building: Burj Khalifa in Dubai (828 m)

Bedouin tents
Stay with the Bedouin people in the Arabian Desert. They live in tents made from goat or camel hair.

Black
Sea

Date
palms

Coffee

Bananas

TURKEY

Caspian
Sea

Persian carpets
Buy a beautiful Persian
carpet in Iran. They're
handmade from thousands
of pieces of wool.

● Aleppo   River
Euphrates

SYRIA

Beirut

Damascus

Hummous

Baklava

Tehran ★

Wheat

IRAN

Pomegranates

Amman

Baghdad ★

River Tigris

IRAQ

● Isfahan

Oil

Dome of
the Rock

Traditional
Arab dress

Basra

Kuwait City ★

KUWAIT

Persian
Gulf

Goats

Burj Al Arab
Hotel

SAUDI
ARABIA

Football

BAHRAIN

Manama

Doha

Traditional
Persian dress

Oil

Riyadh ★

QATAR

Abu
Dhabi

Muscat ★

Red
Sea

● Makkah

UNITED
ARAB
EMIRATES

Olives

Arabian
Sea

Camel racing

OMAN

Coral
reefs

Sana'a ★

YEMEN

Mud-brick
buildings

Fishing

SOCOTRA

45

CENTRAL ASIA

Central Asia has vast plains, huge deserts and towering mountains. Much of the land is too hilly or dry for farming, and many of the countries in the region are quite poor.

Aral Sea
Visit the Aral Sea – while you can. It's shrinking fast as water is drained from it for watering fields.

Space Centre
Watch a rocket blast off at Baikonur Cosmodrome in Kazakhstan. It's the home of Russia's space programme.

Caspian Sea caviar
Taste some caviar (fish eggs) from the Caspian Sea. It comes from a fish called the sturgeon.

Silk Road
Follow the Silk Road (an old trade route), stopping off at ancient cities such as Samarkand.

Oil

Beshbarmak noodles

Obi non flatbread

Aral Sea

Kara Desert

Caspian Sea

TURKMENISTAN

Melons

Ashgabat

Rock carvings
Explore the rock carvings at Tamgaly Gorge in Kazakhstan. They are thousands of years old.

Palace of Peace and Reconciliation

Bayterek Tower

Burana Tower

Astana ★

Baikonur Cosmodrome

Qaraghandy ●

Coal mining

Dombras

Horses

KAZAKHSTAN

Lake Balkhash

Tamgaly rock carvings

Green tea

Syr Darya River

Falconry

Almaty ●

Amu Darya River

Bishkek ★

Lake Issyk-Kul

UZBEKISTAN

Tashkent ★

KYRGYZSTAN

Samarkand

Bukhara ●

Samarkand – historic city

ural gas

TAJIKISTAN

Manti dumplings

Cotton

Dushanbe ★

Kara Kum
Explore the enormous Kara Kum Desert in Turkmenistan. Its name means 'Black Sand'.

Kite fighting

Traditional Tajik dress

★ Kabul

AFGHANISTAN

Kabuli palaw

Kandahar ●

Carpets

FAST FACTS

Biggest country: Kazakhstan
Biggest city: Tashkent, Uzbekistan
Longest river: Syr Darya
Largest desert: Kara Kum, Turkmenistan
Most expensive food: Caviar

SOUTHERN ASIA

The southern part of Asia is crowded and full of colour. There are many different religions and cultures, with festivals almost every day. India is the biggest country in Southern Asia.

Bollywood
Catch a film in India. Hundreds of action-packed films are made in 'Bollywood' every year.

FAST FACTS

Biggest city: Mumbai, India
Smallest country: Bhutan
Holiest river: River Ganges
Most popular religion: Hinduism
Most popular sport: Cricket

Chapatis

PAKISTAN

Kebabs

Karach

Monsoon
Have your umbrella ready. In summer, it pours down with rain. This is called the monsoon.

Hindu gods
Most people in India are Hindus. They worship many gods, such as Ganesh, the elephant god.

Elephant parade
Watch decorated elephants parade through the streets of Kandy in Sri Lanka at festival time.

Archery
Pick up a bamboo bow and arrow, and have a go at archery. It's the national sport of Bhutan.

River Indus

Pakistan Monument

★ Islamabad

Lahore ●

Cricket

Golden Temple

New Delhi ★

Yoga

● Agra

Samosas

INDIA

Mumbai ●

Bollywood

Saris

Arabian Sea

Lassi

Chennai

Bangalore ●

Tea

Sapphires

Indian Ocean

Colombo ★ ● Kandy   SRI LANKA

Sherpas

NEPAL

Kathmandu ★

Butter tea

River Ganges

Kathakali dancing

BHUTAN

★ Thimphu

Rickshaws

Lalbagh Fort

Dhaka ★

Kolkata ●

Brahmaputa River

● Chittagong

BANGLADESH

Bay of Bengal

Taj Mahal
Be amazed by the Taj Mahal in Agra, India. This marble tomb was built by an Indian emperor in memory of his wife.

Gers

Stay in a ger, a traditional Mongolian tent. More than one-third of Mongolia's people live as nomadic herders.

Archery

Sheep

Morin Khuur

Ulaanbaatar

MONGOLIA

Horse riding

Wonton dumplings

Chinese swords

Noodles

Great Wall of China

Wheat

Leshan Giant Buddha

Yellow Riv

Xi'an

Yak racing

Thukpa soup

Yangtze River

Chongqing

CHIN

Three Gorges Dam

Electronic gadgets

FAST FACTS

Biggest country: China
Most crowded city: Hong Kong, China
Least crowded country: Mongolia
Most spoken language: Mandarin Chinese
Fastest train: Maglev bullet train, Japan

Bird's Nest Stadium

Visit the Bird's Nest Stadium in Beijing where the Olympic Games were held in 2008.

CHINA AND ITS NEIGHBOURS

China is an enormous country. More than 1.3 billion people live there – more than in any other country. Its neighbours are Mongolia, North Korea, South Korea and Japan.

Copper

Silk

Khuushuur dumplings

Harbin Ice Festival

Forbidden City

Beijing

Rice paddies

NORTH KOREA

Sea of Japan

Sushi

Bullet trains

Pacific Ocean

Pyongyang

SOUTH KOREA

Seoul

Table tennis

Yellow Sea

Tae kwon do

JAPAN

Osaka

Tokyo

Cherry blossom

Oolong tea

Shanghai

East China Sea

Taipei

TAIWAN

angzhou

ong Kong

South China Sea

Sumo wrestling
Watch sumo wrestling in Japan. The wrestlers try to throw each other to the ground or out of the ring.

Terracotta Army
This army of life-sized clay soldiers was made 2,000 years ago to guard the Emperor's tomb, near Xi'an.

Chinese New Year
Celebrate Chinese New Year with dragon dancing, lanterns and special festival food.

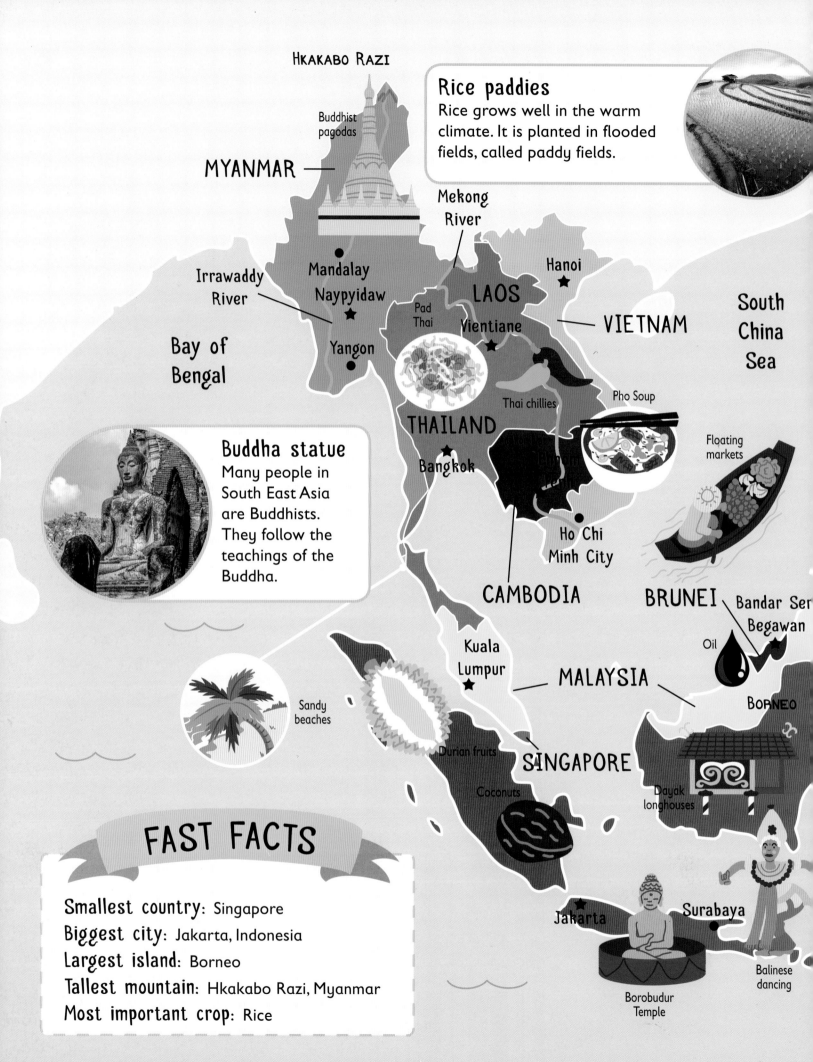

Hkakabo Razi

Buddhist pagodas

MYANMAR

Rice paddies
Rice grows well in the warm climate. It is planted in flooded fields, called paddy fields.

Mekong River

Irrawaddy River

Mandalay
Naypyidaw

Hanoi

LAOS

Pad Thai

Vientiane

VIETNAM

South China Sea

Bay of Bengal

Yangon

Thai chillies

Pho Soup

THAILAND

Buddha statue
Many people in South East Asia are Buddhists. They follow the teachings of the Buddha.

Bangkok

Phnom Penh

Floating markets

Ho Chi Minh City

CAMBODIA

BRUNEI

Bandar Seri Begawan

Oil

Kuala Lumpur

MALAYSIA

BORNEO

Sandy beaches

Durian fruits

SINGAPORE

Dayak longhouses

Coconuts

FAST FACTS

Jakarta

Surabaya

Balinese dancing

Borobudur Temple

Smallest country: Singapore
Biggest city: Jakarta, Indonesia
Largest island: Borneo
Tallest mountain: Hkakabo Razi, Myanmar
Most important crop: Rice

SOUTH EAST ASIA

South East Asia is made up of the mainland and thousands of islands in the Pacific Ocean. The region is hot and rainy all year round. The biggest country is Indonesia.

Angkor Wat
Wander around the magnificent temple of Angkor Wat. It's deep in the Cambodian jungle.

PHILIPPINES

Manila

Basketball

Petronas Towers
See the sky-scraping Petronas Towers in Kuala Lumpur, Malaysia. They're 452 metres tall.

Pacific Ocean

Adobo

Shadow puppets
Watch a puppet show in Indonesia. The puppets tell stories about gods from the Hindu religion.

Rubies

Spices

Palm oil

INDONESIA

Satay

Dili

EAST TIMOR

Timor Sea

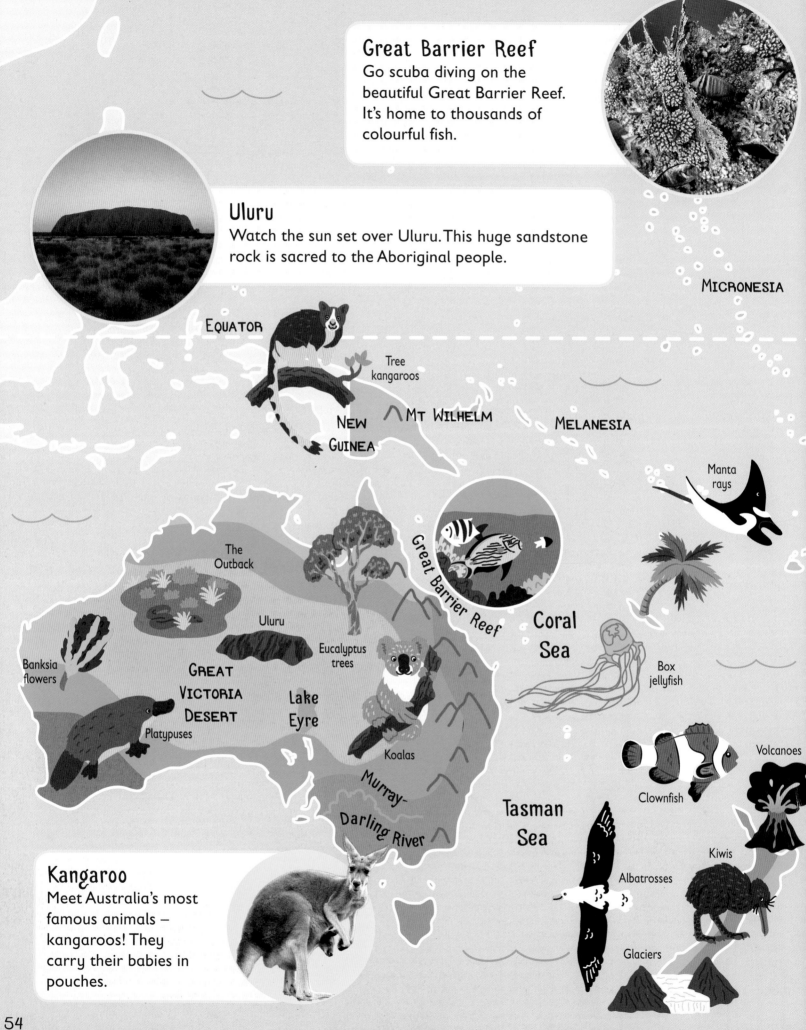

Great Barrier Reef
Go scuba diving on the beautiful Great Barrier Reef. It's home to thousands of colourful fish.

Uluru
Watch the sun set over Uluru. This huge sandstone rock is sacred to the Aboriginal people.

MICRONESIA

EQUATOR

Tree kangaroos

Mt Wilhelm

MELANESIA

NEW GUINEA

Manta rays

Great Barrier Reef

Coral Sea

The Outback

Banksia flowers

GREAT VICTORIA DESERT

Platypuses

Uluru

Eucalyptus trees

Lake Eyre

Koalas

Box jellyfish

Murray-Darling River

Tasman Sea

Clownfish

Volcanoes

Kiwis

Albatrosses

Glaciers

Kangaroo
Meet Australia's most famous animals – kangaroos! They carry their babies in pouches.

FAST FACTS

Size: 8.5 million square kilometres
Population: 40 million
Number of countries: 14
Biggest country: Australia
Smallest country: Nauru

Highest mountain: Mt Wilhelm,
  Papua New Guinea
Longest river: Murray-Darling, Australia
Largest lake: Lake Eyre, Australia
Biggest desert: Great Victoria Desert
Largest coral reef: Great Barrier Reef

Humpback whales

Bird of paradise
Go bird-of-paradise spotting on the island of New Guinea. They're known for their fabulous feathers.

Green sea turtles

POLYNESIA

Sunfish

Pacific
Ocean

Geyser
Watch a geyser erupt in New Zealand, where boiling water bursts up from underground.

OCEANIA

Oceania is a huge region. It is made up of the continent of Australia and hundreds of other smaller islands in the Pacific Ocean. This fascinating region has rainforests, deserts, mountains, volcanoes and the biggest coral reef in the world.

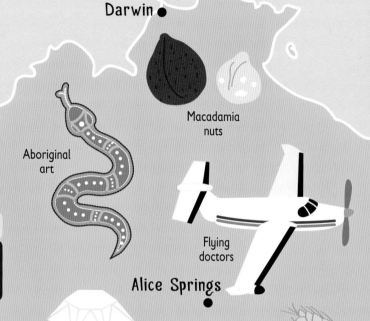

Macadamia
nuts

Opal mining
Precious gemstones called opals are mined in Australia. They shimmer in the light.

Aboriginal
art

Flying
doctors

Alice Springs
•

AUSTRALIA

Vegemite

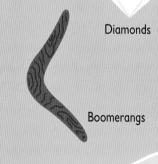

Gold mining

Diamonds

Wheat

Lake
Eyre

Indian
Ocean

Sandy
beaches

Boomerangs

Cricket

Perth
•

Murra

Adelaide •

Darl
Ri

Sydney Opera House
Visit the Opera House in Sydney Harbour. Its roof is designed to look like a ship's sails.

AUSTRALIA
AND NEW ZEALAND

Australia is the biggest country in Oceania. A large part of Australia is dry, dusty desert, so most people live near the coast. To the south-east lie the islands of New Zealand.

Southern
Ocean

Australian Rules
In Australian Rules football, a player can punch or kick the ball but cannot throw it.

Pacific
Ocean

Coral
Sea

Scuba diving

Lamington
cakes

FAST FACTS

Biggest city: Sydney
Main language: English
Most popular sport: Australian Rules football
Biggest cattle farm: Anna Creek Station, Australia
Longest road: Highway 1, Australia

Brisbane ●

Sydney
Opera
House

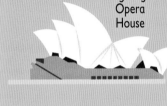

Bungee jumping
Try bungee jumping or white-water rafting in New Zealand – if you're feeling brave!

Parliament
House

● Sydney

★ Canberra

● Melbourne

Surfing

Tasman
Sea

Auckland
●

Sky
Tower

Rugby
union

NORTH
ISLAND

★ Wellington

Hiking

Kiwi fruit

● Christchurch

TASMANIA
Hobart
●

Maoris
The Maoris have lived in New Zealand for thousands of years, and have their own language and culture.

NEW
ZEALAND

● Dunedin

SOUTH
ISLAND

People of Papua
Papua New Guinea is home to hundreds of tribes. They speak more than 700 languages.

MARSHALL ISLANDS

PALAU

★ Majuro

FEDERATED STATES OF MICRONESIA

Breadfruit

KIRIBATI

★ Tarawa

PAPUA NEW GUINEA

NAURU

Land diving

SOLOMON ISLANDS

Copper mining

★ Port Moresby

★ Honiara

VANUATU

FIJI

GREAT BARRIER REEF

Coral Sea

NEW CALEDONIA

Suva ★

Cassava

★ Port Vila

Tabua whale tooth ornament

FAST FACTS

Largest island: New Guinea
Biggest city: Port Moresby, Papua New Guinea
Most popular sport: Rugby
Important crops: Palm oil, coconut, cocoa
Top holiday spot: Fiji

Fiji
With its white, sandy beaches and warm weather, Fiji is a popular place for holidays.

PACIFIC ISLANDS

Hundreds of tiny islands are scattered across the Pacific Ocean. Many are made from coral or are the tops of undersea volcanoes. Around 9 million people live on the Pacific Islands.

Lavalava (kilt)

Pacific Ocean

Rugby union

Lap lap
Try a plate of lap lap from Vanuatu. It's mashed yam mixed with meat and fresh coconut cream.

Equator

Taro

International Date Line

Coconut crabs

Coconuts

SAMOA

Apia ★

COOK ISLANDS

AMERICAN SAMOA

FRENCH POLYNESIA

TONGA

Bark cloth

Canoe trip
Get paddling! Traditionally, the Pacific Islanders carved dugout canoes from large trees.

Date line
Check the calendar as the date changes at the International Date Line. It runs down the Pacific Ocean.

Husky sled
Drive a husky sled across the ice with the Inuit people or hitch a lift on a snowmobile.

Oil

Icebreakers

Arctic Circle

Icebergs

Midnight Sun
In summer, it never gets dark in the Arctic. The sun stays high in the sky all day and night long.

● North Pole

Arctic foxes

Arctic terns

Walruses

Novaya Zemlya

Arctic Ocean

Svalbard

Narwhals

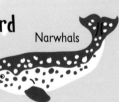

Inuit people

Greenland

Polar bears
Follow a polar bear on the ice as it hunts for seals. Its thick fur helps to keep it warm.

THE ARCTIC

The icy Arctic is the area around the North Pole at the far north of Earth. It is mostly made up of the frozen Arctic Ocean, and includes the lands that surround it.

ANTARCTICA

At the southern end of Earth, Antarctica is the coldest, windiest continent. It is surrounded by the stormy Southern Ocean. The ocean freezes over in winter.

Scientists

Scientists are the only people to live in Antarctica. They study the weather, ice and wildlife.

Emperor penguins

Hardy emperor penguins breed on the ice in the middle of the freezing Antarctic winter.

Blue whales

Icebreakers

Halley Research Station

Leopard seals

Antarctic Peninsula

Ronne Ice Shelf

Amundsen-Scott South Pole Station

Southern Ocean

Antarctic Circle

South Pole

Transantarctic Mountains

Lake Vostok

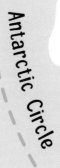

Elephant seals

Ross Ice Shelf

Mt. Erebus

Penguins

Orcas

FAST FACTS

Size: around 14 million square kilometres

Lowest temperature: -94.7 °C

First person to reach South Pole: Roald Amundsen, 1911

Most famous animal: Penguin

Biggest ice shelf: Ross Ice Shelf

Mt Erebus

Watch Mt Erebus erupt — from a safe distance! It is the most southerly volcano in the world.

QUIZ TIME!

Now you've completed your journey around the world, see if you know the answers to these questions. If you're not sure, take another look at the maps to find the answers.

1. Which is the biggest continent?
   a) Africa
   b) Asia
   c) Antarctica

2. Where do giant pandas live?
   a) France
   b) Mexico
   c) China

3. Who built Machu Picchu?
   a) The Incas
   b) The Aztecs
   c) The Ancient Egyptians

4. Where can you climb Mt Kilimanjaro?
   a) Europe
   b) Africa
   c) Antarctica

5. Who lives at the South Pole?
   a) Polar bears
   b) Walruses
   c) Scientists

6. Bandy is a popular sport in which country?
   a) Bolivia
   b) Belgium
   c) Russia

7. Which is the main language spoken in Mexico and Central America?
   a) Spanish
   b) German
   c) English

8. Where might you look for the legendary Loch Ness Monster?
   a) Brazil
   b) Scotland
   c) Nigeria

INDEX